Nature's Cycles
Food Chains

Dana Meachen Rau

Marshall Cavendish
Benchmark
New York

2

Running! Jumping! Playing! Where do you get all your *energy*? You get energy for your body from food.

All living things need food.
Food is a type of energy.
A *food chain* is the flow of
energy from one living thing
to the next.

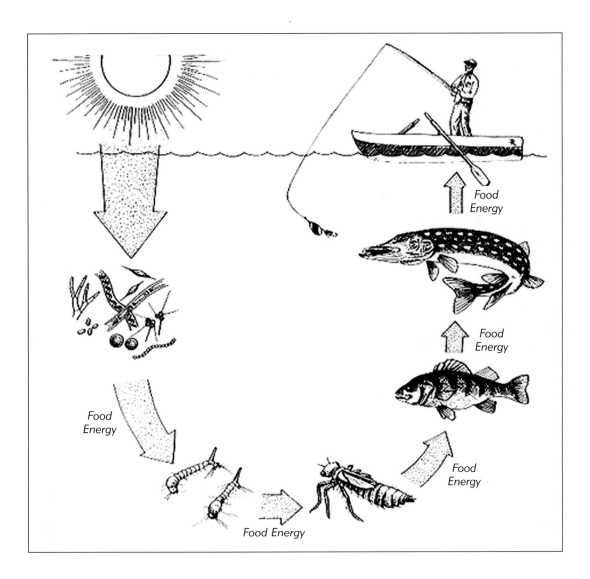

Food Energy

Food Energy

Food Energy

Food Energy

Food Energy

5

Plants make their own food. Their leaves take in energy from the sun.

Their roots suck water and
nutrients from the *soil*. They take
a gas out of the air. Plants use
all these things to make food.

Animals cannot make their own food. They need to find food to eat so they can live.

Some animals eat plants to get energy. Cows and horses eat grass.

Pandas feed on stalks
of bamboo.

Some animals eat meat to get energy. Spiders catch flies in webs.

Snakes hunt for mice. Vultures eat animals that have died.

Some animals eat both plants and animals. Berries and fish are food for a bear. Nuts and crabs can feed a raccoon. Kids eat plants and animals, too. The food you eat gives you energy.

All living things die. Plants turn brown and fall to the ground.

Animals do not live forever
either. Some animals are eaten
by other animals. Other animals
die when they get old.

Dead plants and animals *decay*. Mushrooms grow on a dead log. They help turn the log into soil. The soil is rich with nutrients. New plants use the nutrients to grow.

Animals that hunt and eat
other animals are *predators*.
The animals they eat are *prey*.

No one eats the top predator in a food chain. The predator will die and decay. Its energy is given back to the soil.

Look at a food chain in a pond.
A fish eats plants.

An alligator eats the fish.
When the alligator dies, it falls
to the bottom. When it decays,
it helps new plants grow.

Look at a food chain in a field.
A cricket eats grass.

A bird eats the cricket. The bird
dies and decays. This feeds the
soil so the grass can grow.

In food chains, different animals eat the same foods. A predator may eat more than one kind of plant or animal. The food chains mix together. This is a *food web*.

Living things need each other. When they die, they help other living things grow.

Challenge Words

decay (DEE-kay)—To break down into nutrients for the soil.

energy (EN-uhr-jee)—The power to do work.

food chain—The flow of energy from one living thing to the next.

food web—The criss-cross flow of energy among animals and plants in an area.

nutrients (NOO-tree-ehnts)—A food material needed for growth.

predator (PRED-uh-tuhr)—An animal that hunts and eats other animals.

prey (pray)—An animal that is eaten by another animal.

soil—The earth in which plants grow.

Index

Page numbers in **boldface** are illustrations.

The author would like to thank Paula Meachen
for her scientific guidance and expertise in reviewing this book.

With thanks to Nanci Vargus, Ed.D., and Beth Walker Gambro, reading consultants

Marshall Cavendish Benchmark
99 White Plains Road
Tarrytown, New York 10591-9001
www.marshallcavendish.us

Library of Congress Cataloging-in-Publication Data

Rau, Dana Meachen, 1971–
Food chains / by Dana Meachen Rau.
p. cm. — (Bookworms. Nature's cycles)
Includes index.
Summary: "Introduces the idea that many things in the world around us
are cyclical in nature and explores the food chain"—Provided by publisher.
ISBN 978-0-7614-4095-6
1. Food chains (Ecology)—Juvenile literature. I. Title.
QH541.14.R38 2009
577'.16—dc22
2008042508

Editor: Christina Gardeski
Publisher: Michelle Bisson
Designer: Virginia Pope
Art Director: Anahid Hamparian

Photo Research by Anne Burns Images

Cover Photo by *Photo Researchers*/Linda Freshwaters Amdt

The photographs in this book are used with permission and through the courtesy of:
Animals Animals: pp. 1, 25 ABPL Gerald Hinde. *Getty Images*: p. 2 Sabine Scheckel; p. 6 James French;
p. 8 Anup Shak; p. 10 Richard Ross; p. 11 Keren Su; p. 17 Andrew Holt; p. 19 Tim Graham; p. 20 Getty Images;
p. 21 Time & Life Pictures. *Photri Microstock*: p. 5. *Photo Researchers*: p. 7 Gunilla Elam; p. 16 Nigel Cattlin;
p. 23 James H. Robinson; p. 24 Hans Reinhard; p. 27 Linda Freshwaters Amdt; p. 28 Clem Haagner. *Corbis*:
p. 12 Herbert Kehrer/zefa; p. 13 David A. Northcott. *Photo Edit*: p. 14 Richard Hutchings. *Peter Arnold*: p. 22 BIOS.

Printed in Malaysia
1 3 5 6 4 2